Korene
VandenBerg
12/15/09

If I Could Be.

Written by: Korene Boulter (5th Grade)
Illustrated by: Korene VandenBerg

RoseDog Books
PITTSBURGH, PENNSYLVANIA 15222

The contents of this work including, but not limited to, the accuracy of events, people, and places depicted; opinions expressed; permission to use previously published materials included; and any advice given or actions advocated are solely the responsibility of the author, who assumes all liability for said work and indemnifies the publisher against any claims stemming from publication of the work

Permission for the reproduction and adaptation of the illustration from *Who is the Beast?* by Keith Baker, copyright © 1990 by The Trumpet Club, provided by Houghton Mifflin Harcourt Publishing Company.

ISBN: 978-1-4349-9381-6
Printed in the United States of America

First Printing

For information or to order additional books, please write:
RoseDog Books
701 Smithfield St.
Pittsburgh, PA 15222
U.S.A.
1-800-834-1803
Or visit our web site and
on-line bookstore at www.rosedogbookstore.com

This book is dedicated to my sons, Canton and Maxwell.
Always be proud of who you are.

Thanks Mom for saving this poem and all of the twenty-million other items you have saved through the years.

If I could be a rabbit slick,

I could beat a turtle quick.

If I could be a tiger sly,

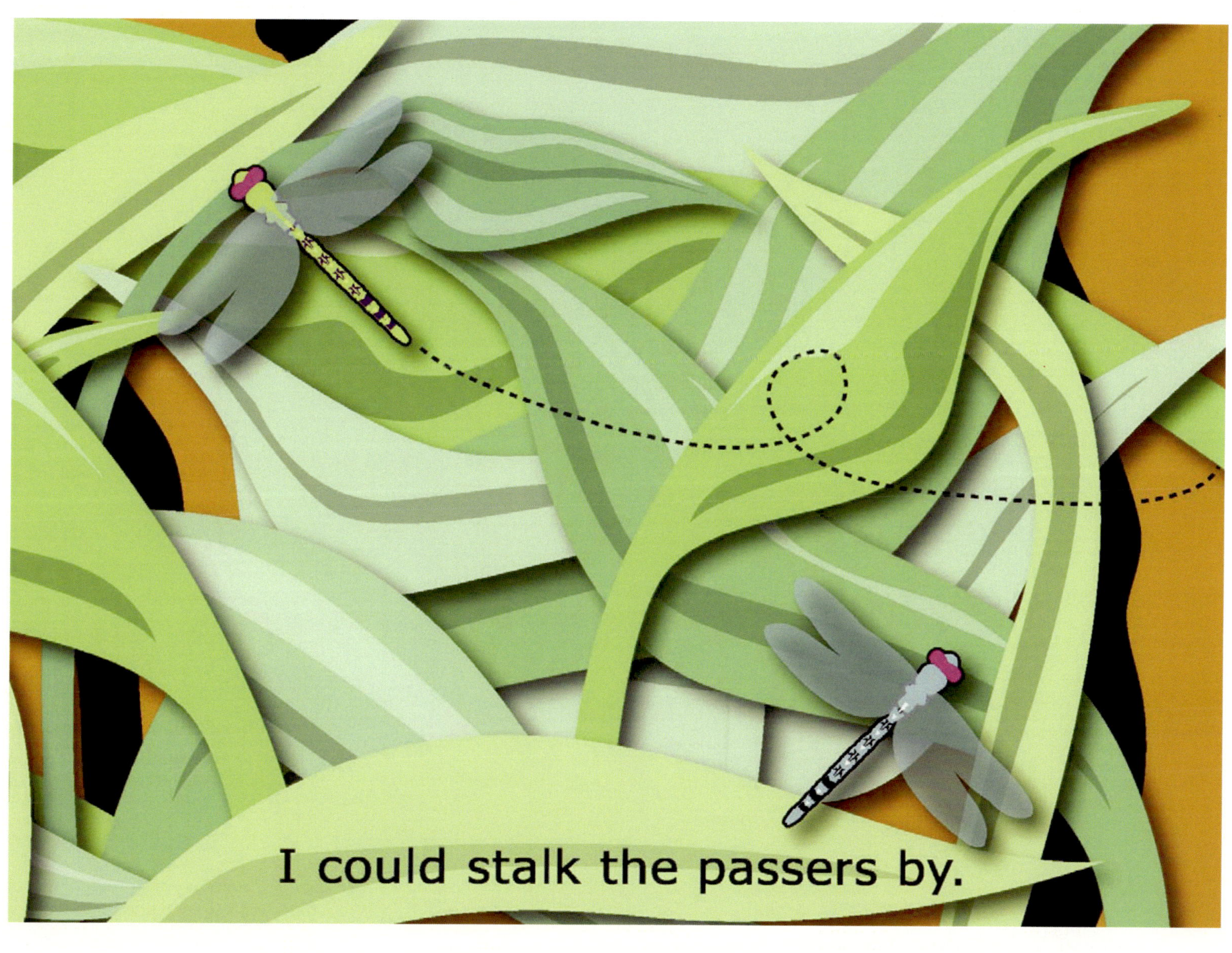
I could stalk the passers by.

If I could be a big black bear,

I could have lots of furry hair.

If I could be a worm so slow,

I could watch the dandelions grow.

But, me I'm proud to be.

Yes, I’m just glad I’m me!

About the Author – Korene VandenBerg lives on a dirt road in Western Michigan with her husband, John, and two sons, Canton and Maxwell.

She and her husband discovered their oldest son had neurological issues in the fall of 2006. He was struggling with school and social interactions. So Korene and her husband decided that one of them would have to stay home to work with their son and take him to therapy. As a result, the household income took a hit. The family made the most of the situation, though, by getting creative. For instance, Korene gave this book to her two sons one Christmas. It is a poem she wrote in fifth grade that her mom had saved. Korene developed illustrations to create the book in its present form.

Can you find Canton and Maxwell on the last page? Even though all the children are unique in their own special way – there's two boys who have one totally different characteristic, than all the other children.

Hint: It's in their smile.